MY FIRST POCKET GUIDE

BACKYARD WILDERNESS

Consultants : David W. Inouye, Ronald M. Nowak, George E. Watson
Illustrators: Wendy Smith, Theophilus Britt Griswold

Published by
The National Geographic Society
John M. Fahey, Jr., President and Chief Executive Officer
Gilbert M. Grosvenor, Chairman of the Board
Nina D. Hoffman, Senior Vice President
William R. Gray, Vice President and Director, Book Division

Staff for this Book
Barbara Brownell, Director of Continuities
Marianne R. Koszorus, Senior Art Director
Toni Eugene, Editor
Alexandra Littlehales, Art Director
Catherine Herbert Howell, Writer-Researcher
Susan V. Kelly, Illustrations Editor
Sharon Kocsis Berry, Illustrations Assistant
Mark A. Caraluzzi, Director of Direct Response Marketing
Heidi Vincent, Product Manager
Vincent P. Ryan, Manufacturing Manager
Lewis R. Bassford, Production Project Manager

Visit our Web site at www.nationalgeographic.com

Library of Congress Catalog Card Number: 99-70468
ISBN: 0-7922-3462-6

Color separations by Quad Graphics, Martinsburg, West Virginia
Printed in Mexico by R.R. Donnelley & Sons Company

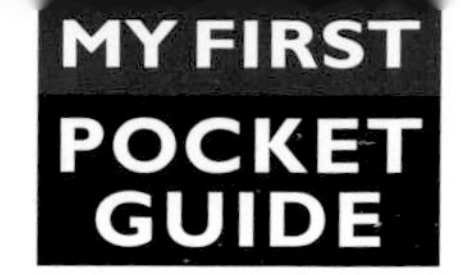

BACKYARD WILDERNESS

CATHERINE HERBERT HOWELL

All photographs supplied by Animals Animals/Earth Scenes

NATIONAL
GEOGRAPHIC
SOCIETY

INTRODUCTION

Whether your backyard is 50 acres in the country or 500 square feet in the city, it is a wilderness for you to explore. You may have seen birds and butterflies, squirrels and spiders, but there is probably a whole lot more going on that you have never seen or thought about!

In this book you will learn about a variety of creatures that may live in your backyard wilderness. Many of the kinds of animals we show here—from mammals to insects—occur throughout much of North America. If a certain species does not live in your area, a similar one probably does. For example, if an eastern cottontail doesn't live where you do, perhaps a desert cottontail does instead. Be creative as you seek the creatures around you.

HOW TO USE THIS BOOK

The animals in this book are arranged according to the level at which they spend much of their time: Underground, ground level, above ground in bushes and shrubs, and in trees. Within each level animals are presented from biggest to smallest. Vertebrates, or animals with backbones, are described first. Invertebrates, or animals without backbones, follow. Each spread helps you identify one kind of animal. A paw print or hoof print indicates the track made by a mammal. A shaded map of North America shows where to find each animal, and the "Field Notes" entry gives an additional fact about it. If you see a word you don't know, look it up in the Glossary on page 76.

EASTERN CHIPMUNK

UNDERGROUND

Streaking through fallen leaves, an eastern chipmunk disappears into its underground burrow. It deposits a mouthful of seeds and berries there to eat in winter.

FIELD NOTES

This little mammal can store more than a hundred seeds at a time in its expandable cheek pouches.

Chipmunks often raid each other's burrows and steal from the food supplies stored in them.

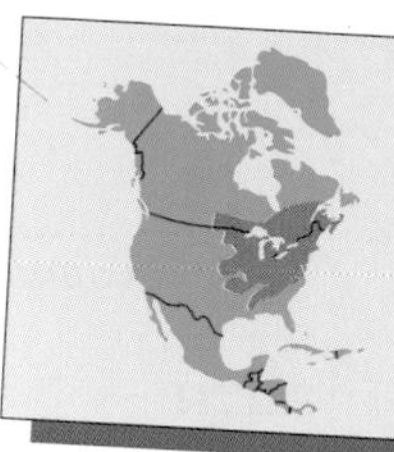

WHERE TO FIND:

The eastern chipmunk lives in wooded and brushy areas in southeastern Canada and most of the United States.

WHAT TO LOOK FOR:

✱ SIZE
Chipmunks measure about nine inches long, including a three-inch tail.

✱ COLOR
They have reddish brown bodies with cream and black stripes on their sides.

✱ BEHAVIOR
Chipmunks sleep much of the winter in an underground nest chamber.

✱ MORE
They wake from time to time to eat their stored food.

EARTHWORM

The slimy, wriggly earthworm is a backyard hero. It tunnels through soil, helping to mix it up and bring in oxygen. It eats leaves and other debris. Then these pass out of its body, making the soil richer.

WHERE TO FIND:
Earthworms live in moist soil throughout nearly all North America, even in Arctic regions.

WHAT TO LOOK FOR:

✱ SIZE
Earthworms range from one to eight inches in length.

✱ COLOR
Most earthworms are pinkish brown.

✱ BEHAVIOR
The rings, or segments, of a worm's body allow it to twist and to move forward and backward.

✱ MORE
Up to 50,000 earthworms may inhabit one acre of moist soil.

Earthworms have mouths but lack other common features such as eyes, ears, and noses.

COMMON BLACK GROUND BEETLE

By day, common black ground beetles hide under rocks and logs. By night, these insects with armor-like forewings hunt caterpillars, earthworms, and other squishy prey.

FIELD NOTES

These beetles lay eggs underground that hatch into soft-bodied young called larvae (LAR-vee).

Some 3,000 different kinds of ground beetles live in North America.

WHERE TO FIND:

Common black ground beetles live on and under the ground throughout much of North America.

WHAT TO LOOK FOR:

✱ SIZE
The common black ground beetle is ½ to ⅝ of an inch long.

✱ COLOR
Its body is shiny black.

✱ BEHAVIOR
Ground beetles have two pairs of wings but they seldom fly. Sometimes they climb trees to search for food.

✱ MORE
Their mouthparts work like a knife and fork to carve up their food.

LITTLE BLACK ANT

For tiny insects, little black ants carry heavy loads. Day and night, these ants spend many hours looking for food and then carrying it long distances to their underground colonies.

Little black ants like to eat almost anything humans do, such as this piece of orange.

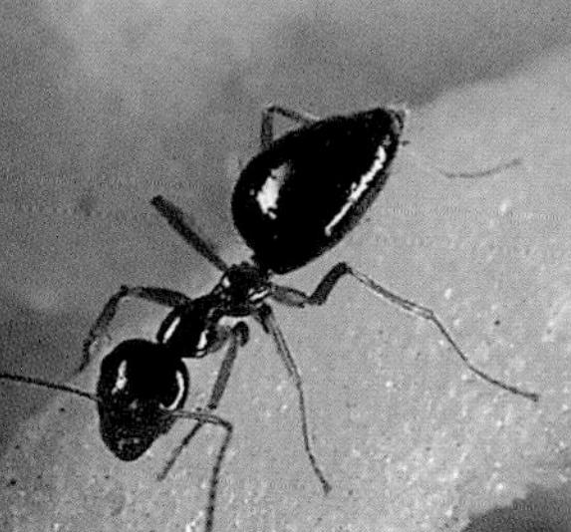

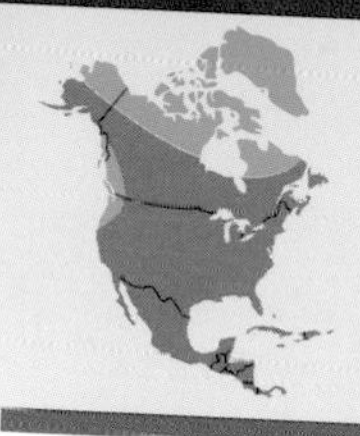

WHERE TO FIND:
Little black ants live in nearly all land habitats throughout much of North America.

WHAT TO LOOK FOR:

✱ SIZE
These ants are about 1⁄16 of an inch long—half the size of a grain of rice.

✱ COLOR
They are shiny black or dark brown.

✱ BEHAVIOR
Each ant in a colony has a specific job to perform.

✱ MORE
Like all insects, ants have a three-part body. A "waist" between the second and third sections gives ants a distinctive shape.

WHITE-TAILED DEER

White-tailed deer live at ground level. Morning and evening, these mammals come to the edge of the woods to feed on grass and twigs. They also visit backyards.

WHERE TO FIND:
The white-tailed deer is found in woods and forests in most of North America, from Canada southward.

WHAT TO LOOK FOR:

✷ SIZE
Adult males are three feet high at the shoulder. Females are a bit smaller.

✷ COLOR
Adults are grayish in winter and reddish in summer. Young are spotted.

✷ BEHAVIOR
White-tailed deer can run fast—about 40 miles an hour.

✷ MORE
Males grow a set of antlers each year before the mating season.

White-tailed deer will eat almost any kind of vegetation, including garden shrubs and flowers.

FIELD NOTES

As it runs away, the white-tailed deer raises its tail. The underside is white and signals danger.

RACCOON

Looking and acting like a masked bandit, a raccoon may come in the night and trash your trash for food. Raccoons are very much at home in cities as well as in suburbs.

WHERE TO FIND:
Raccoons live on much of the continent, from southern Canada to Central America.

WHAT TO LOOK FOR:

✱ SIZE
Raccoons are the size of small dogs, measuring three feet, including the tail.

✱ COLOR
They are mostly gray, with a white face, a black mask, and a banded tail.

✱ BEHAVIOR
Raccoons make their dens in logs, tree stumps, and often in attics.

✱ MORE
They are usually experts in opening garbage cans to get at food inside.

Raccoons have very sensitive fingers. They can find food just by feeling it, especially in the water.

FIELD NOTES

Raccoons are good swimmers, going in after fish and crayfish. They also swim to escape enemies.

VIRGINIA OPOSSUM

The Virginia opossum moves slowly, dragging its tail on the ground. Opossums are North America's only marsupial (mar-SOO-pee-uhl), or pouched mammal.

WHERE TO FIND:

This opossum lives in many places in North America, but rarely in mountains or deserts, or on prairies.

WHAT TO LOOK FOR:

✱ SIZE
Its body is about 20 inches long, not including a 12-inch hairless tail.

✱ COLOR
It is mostly pale gray, with a white face.

✱ BEHAVIOR
The Virginia opossum is active mainly at night, looking for fruit, other plants, and smaller animals to eat.

✱ MORE
Like other marsupials, a baby opossum lives in its mother's pouch.

The Virginia opossum is a good tree climber. A mother often climbs with her babies holding tightly to her back.

FIELD NOTES

When an enemy nears, a Virginia opossum may "play possum"—it may collapse and play dead.

EASTERN COTTONTAIL

GROUND LEVEL

Before she leaves her nest in the ground to look for food, an eastern cottontail rabbit tucks in her babies. She pulls a mat of leaves and grass over them for protection.

Eastern cottontails often rest or hide during the day in a form, a small dent they make in grass or weeds.

WHERE TO FIND:

The eastern cottontail lives in many kinds of habitats from the eastern U.S. through Central America.

WHAT TO LOOK FOR:

✷ SIZE
Eastern cottontails are 17 to 19 inches long, including their fluffy, 2-inch tails.

✷ COLOR
They are brownish gray, with a rust-colored patch on the back of the neck.

✷ BEHAVIOR
Females have up to six litters of as many as eight babies each year.

✷ MORE
Eastern cottontails often take over the burrows of other animals for nests.

FIELD NOTES

Gardeners often find that the cottontail, like Peter Rabbit, eats their vegetables and flowers.

DEER MOUSE

After dark, the deer mouse leaves its cozy nest to search for the berries, seeds, and nuts it loves to eat. It rarely travels far, spending most of its life just a few hundred feet from where it was born.

FIELD NOTES

A deer mouse eats an acorn by hollowing out the center. A kind of acorn "thimble" is all that remains.

Deer mice build nests in hollow logs, tree stumps, and abandoned animal burrows.

WHERE TO FIND:

The deer mouse lives in nearly every land habitat throughout much of the United States and Canada.

WHAT TO LOOK FOR:

✷ SIZE

Including its tail, the deer mouse is about seven inches long.

✷ COLOR

Like the deer for which it was named, this mouse is gray to reddish brown, with white underneath.

✷ BEHAVIOR

It often stores food for the winter.

✷ MORE

A deer mouse also eats insects, worms, spiders, and bird eggs.

SHORT-TAILED SHREW

GROUND LEVEL

Often mistaken for a mouse, the short-tailed shrew is a fierce and hungry creature. Each day it may eat its own weight in small mammals, insects, snails, and invertebrates.

WHERE TO FIND:

Short-tailed shrews live in wooded and damp areas in southeastern Canada and the eastern United States.

WHAT TO LOOK FOR:

✱ SIZE
Short-tailed shrews measure up to four inches long, including their one-inch tails. Some weigh less than a quarter.

✱ COLOR
They are brownish gray.

✱ BEHAVIOR
Male shrews often fight each other for females and for territory.

✱ MORE
After they mate, males and females often stay together.

FIELD NOTES

A short-tailed shrew bites prey in the face, paralyzing it with poisonous saliva before eating it.

If a shrew is very frightened, its heart may beat 1,200 times a minute, often causing it to die from fright.

MOURNING DOVE

GROUND LEVEL

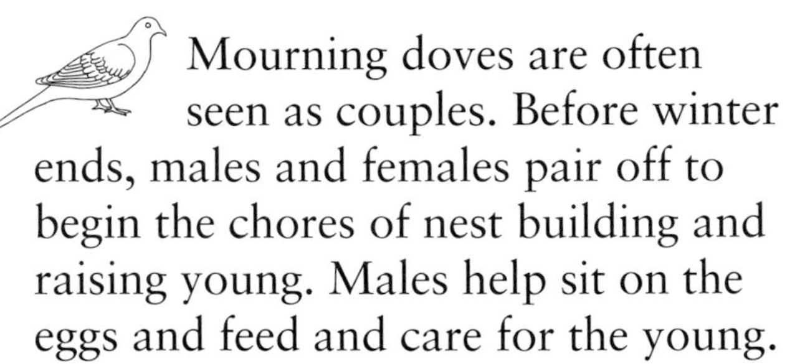

Mourning doves are often seen as couples. Before winter ends, males and females pair off to begin the chores of nest building and raising young. Males help sit on the eggs and feed and care for the young.

WHERE TO FIND:
This dove lives in parks, gardens, and fields from southern Canada through Central America.

WHAT TO LOOK FOR:

✷ SIZE
The doves are about 12 inches long.

✷ COLOR
Their bodies are grayish brown above and pinkish underneath.

✷ BEHAVIOR
Their wings make a fluttering kind of whistle as they take off in flight.

✷ MORE
They get their name from their sad *oowoo-woo-woo-woo* call, which sounds as if they are in mourning.

Mourning doves walk slowly over the ground looking for seeds, their favorite food.

AMERICAN ROBIN

GROUND LEVEL

The American robin does not fear humans. A pair will nest in the middle of a busy garden. They hop around the lawn, looking and listening for worms.

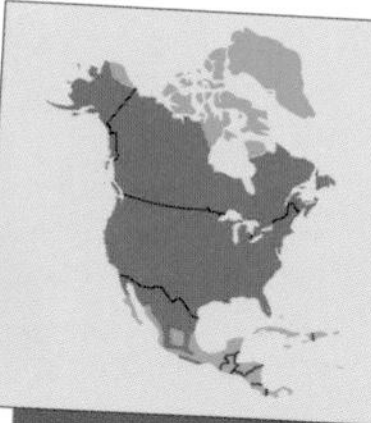

WHERE TO FIND:

The American robin lives in a wide range of habitats throughout most of the North American continent.

WHAT TO LOOK FOR:

✱ SIZE
The American robin measures about ten inches in length.

✱ COLOR
Adults are dark grayish brown above, with bright, reddish brown breasts.

✱ BEHAVIOR
They sing a happy song that sounds like *cheerily cheer-up cheerio.*

✱ MORE
In addition to worms, robins eat insects, berries, and other kinds of fruit.

An adult robin brings a tasty worm to a nest full of hungry nestlings.

TIGER SALAMANDER

GROUND LEVEL

Like other amphibians (am-FIB-ee-uhns), a tiger salamander starts out as an egg laid in water. It hatches into a young animal that lives in water, then moves onto land.

FIELD NOTES

Like Peter Pan, some tiger salamanders never grow up. They live in water their whole lives.

Tiger salamanders eat earthworms, insects, other amphibians, and even mice.

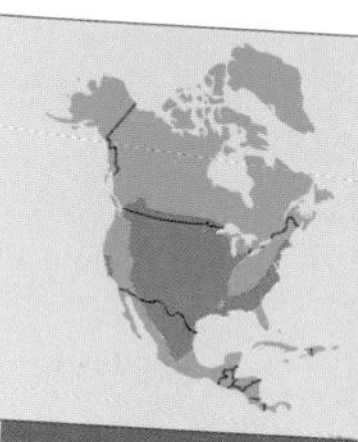

WHERE TO FIND:

Tiger salamanders live throughout the central part of North America, seldom far from water.

WHAT TO LOOK FOR:

✱ SIZE
Tiger salamanders measure 6 to 13 inches long.

✱ COLOR
They are usually dark brown or black, with lighter spots or stripes.

✱ BEHAVIOR
Tiger salamanders often dig burrows as moles do.

✱ MORE
You may see these amphibians at night after a heavy rain.

AMERICAN TOAD

Each spring, the melodic song of the American toad rises from marshes and ponds. Male toads sing by bringing air into their mouths to inflate sacs in their throats. Their trilling lures females for mates.

WHERE TO FIND:

The American toad lives in a number of different habitats in eastern and central North America.

WHAT TO LOOK FOR:

✷ SIZE
Female American toads measure up to four inches long. Males are smaller.

✷ COLOR
American toads are often brown or grayish, with dark blotches.

✷ BEHAVIOR
These amphibians hunt insects, worms, and snails at night, catching them with their long, sticky tongues.

✷ MORE
A toad may eat 10,000 insects a summer.

American toads have colorful bumps on their bodies. Some bumps produce fluids that can poison enemies.

FIELD NOTES

In winter, the American toad burrows into the ground and stays until the weather warms up.

COMMON GARTER SNAKE

The common garter snake is a very common reptile. It glides quietly through the grass, searching for the frogs, toads, and salamanders it eats.

FIELD NOTES

A garter snake can unhinge its jaws so that it can eat prey much larger than it is, such as an egg.

Common garter snakes do not lay eggs as many snakes do. Garter snakes give birth to live young.

WHERE TO FIND:

The common garter snake is found in southern Canada and throughout the United States.

WHAT TO LOOK FOR:

✱ SIZE

Common garter snakes can grow to be 50 inches long.

✱ COLOR

They are usually dark brown or black, often with light stripes on their sides.

✱ BEHAVIOR

In the winter, thousands may gather together in one place to keep warm.

✱ MORE

Common garter snakes are often kept as pets.

MILLIPEDE

Although the word "millipede" means "one thousand legs," no millipede has that many. This invertebrate has two pairs of jointed legs on the several dozen segments of its body, but it cannot move quickly.

WHERE TO FIND:

Millipedes are found in dark and damp places, such as rock crevices, throughout North America.

WHAT TO LOOK FOR:

✱ SIZE
Most millipedes measure from one to five inches in length.

✱ COLOR
They are usually dark brown or black. Some are yellow, and some are red.

✱ BEHAVIOR
They have glands containing smelly liquid that they squirt at enemies.

✱ MORE
Millipedes eat dead and decaying plants and animals.

Since it can't run away, the millipede often hides from its enemies under rocks and logs.

FIELD NOTES

Unlike the millipede, this centipede has only one set of legs on each segment of its body.

GARDEN SNAIL

To get moving, a garden snail must slime itself! It makes a layer of slime under its long foot so it can glide along the ground. The snail scrunches up its foot and stretches it ahead to travel.

FIELD NOTES

This snail lays a mass of hundreds of jelly-like eggs in the ground, then covers them with soil.

The snail's head is on the front end of the foot it pushes out of its shell to travel. The snail's eyes are on top of two tentacles.

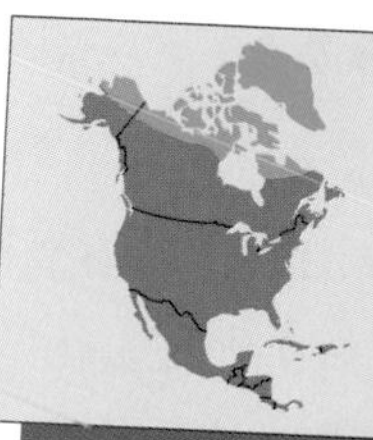

WHERE TO FIND:

Originally from Europe, garden snails are now widespread throughout North America.

WHAT TO LOOK FOR:

✳ SIZE

A garden snail is about 1½ inches in length.

✳ COLOR

Its shell is brownish, with dark stripes.

✳ BEHAVIOR

In the winter, garden snails burrow into soil, sealing themselves in their shells with slime to keep from drying out.

✳ MORE

Just hatched snails are like tiny versions of their parents but have soft shells.

FIELD CRICKET

GROUND LEVEL

You may know that field crickets jump, but did you also know that they dance and sing? Male crickets do both to attract mates. They hop around the females, trilling a high-pitched sound.

WHERE TO FIND:
Field crickets are found on lawns, in woods, in fields, and frequently inside houses in much of North America.

WHAT TO LOOK FOR:

✱ SIZE
A field cricket measures ½ to 1 inch in length.

✱ COLOR
It has a black or reddish brown body.

✱ BEHAVIOR
Females lay their eggs deep in the soil, where they usually remain until they hatch in spring.

✱ MORE
Crickets eat many kinds of plants as well as dead and dying insects.

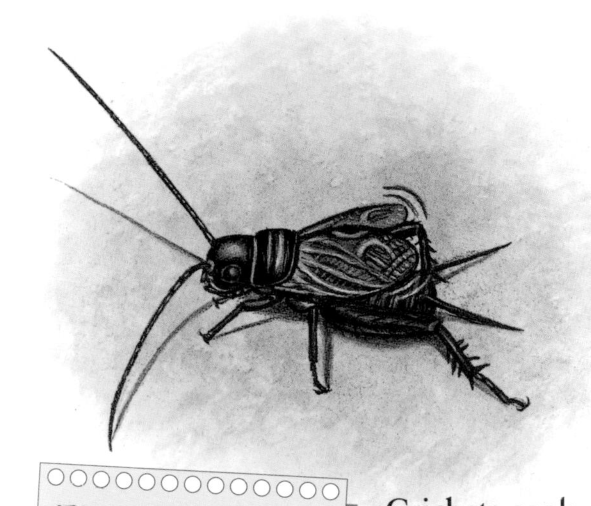

FIELD NOTES

A male field cricket makes his song by rubbing together special places on its front pair of wings.

Crickets soak up the sun. In cold weather, these insects seek shelter, often moving into houses.

PILLBUG

Though it looks like an insect, the pillbug is really a crustacean (krus-TAY-shun), a hard-shelled invertebrate related to crabs and lobsters. Unlike these relatives, the pillbug lives on land.

WHERE TO FIND:

Pillbugs live in dead leaves and woodpiles and under stones, flowerpots, and logs in much of North America.

WHAT TO LOOK FOR:

✳ SIZE
Pillbugs measure up to ½ inch long.

✳ COLOR
They are usually black or gray, with segmented bodies.

✳ BEHAVIOR
Though they live on land, pillbugs prefer damp places.

✳ MORE
Pillbugs feed on dead leaves, bark, and mushrooms and other fungi. Pillbugs are also called wood lice.

FIELD NOTES

The pillbug's habit of rolling up into a ball when it is disturbed has earned it the nickname roly-poly.

Like other crustaceans, a pillbug has two pairs of antennae on its head, one of them very tiny.

LADYBIRD BEETLE

The nursery rhyme tells the ladybird beetle, or ladybug, to "fly away home." You should hope that it makes a home in your yard, where it will eat plant pests.

There are more than 3,000 kinds of ladybugs with many different patterns.

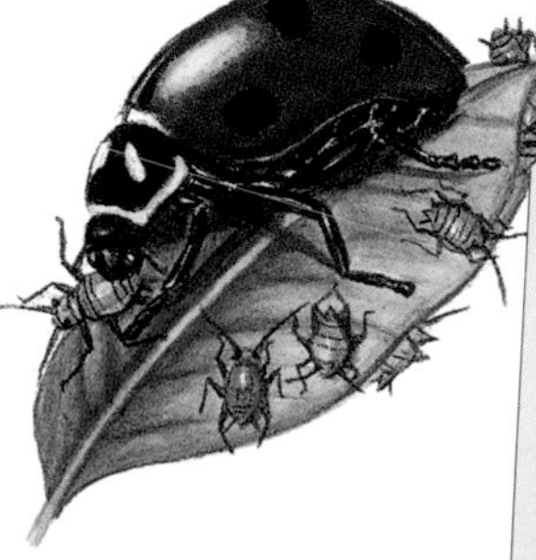

FIELD NOTES

Ladybugs devour aphids (AY-fids), a kind of tiny insect that sucks the juices from plants, killing them.

WHERE TO FIND:
Ladybird beetles live on the leaves of many different plants throughout much of North America.

WHAT TO LOOK FOR:

✱ SIZE
Ladybugs are 1/16 to 1/4 of an inch long, the size of chocolate chips.

✱ COLOR
They are mostly red, orange, or yellow with black spots.

✱ BEHAVIOR
Thousands of ladybugs may spend the winter together under leaves or bark.

✱ MORE
Ladybug young, called larvae, also feed on aphids.

HOUSE WREN

BUSH-AND-SHRUB LEVEL

A male house wren is like a real estate agent. He begins building several nests, often at the level of bushes and shrubs, then takes the female on tour to inspect them. They move into her favorite and finish it.

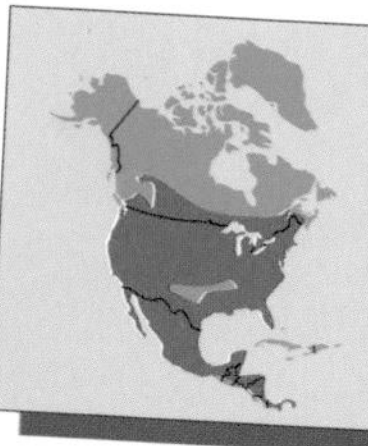

WHERE TO FIND:
House wrens are common in gardens, parks, and farmland throughout much of North America.

WHAT TO LOOK FOR:

✷ SIZE
House wrens measure almost five inches in length.

✷ COLOR
They are mostly brown, with darker bars on their backs.

✷ BEHAVIOR
House wrens have a very cheery song, a series of bubbling musical notes.

✷ MORE
They use their thin, pointy bills to snatch up insects.

These birds often nest in holes in hollow trees. They also use man-made wren houses.

FIELD NOTES

A male house wren labors to build a fine nest inside a mailbox. Wrens use a variety of objects as shelters.

BLACK-CAPPED CHICKADEE

BUSH-AND-SHRUB LEVEL

A backyard acrobat, the black-capped chickadee flits around singing its name, *chick-a-dee-dee-dee*. Chickadees of different kinds are found all over the continent.

WHERE TO FIND:
Black-capped chickadees live in wooded areas throughout central North America.

WHAT TO LOOK FOR:

✱ **SIZE**
The black-capped chickadee measures about five inches long.

✱ **COLOR**
It is gray and white, with a black cap and bib.

✱ **BEHAVIOR**
In winter small groups of chickadees may roam in search of backyard feeders.

✱ **MORE**
The birds eat insects, seeds, and berries with their little bills.

Black-capped chickadees are some of the boldest visitors to backyard bird feeders. Their antics are very entertaining.

FIELD NOTES

Feeding upside down, or in other awkward positions, doesn't seem to bother the black-capped chickadee.

MONARCH BUTTERFLY

Bush-and-Shrub Level

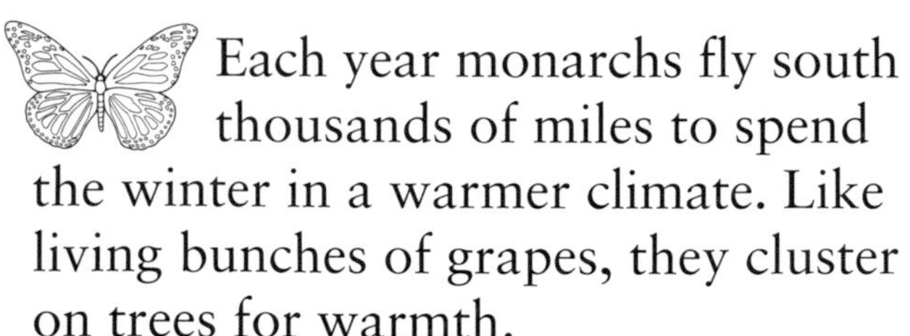

Each year monarchs fly south thousands of miles to spend the winter in a warmer climate. Like living bunches of grapes, they cluster on trees for warmth.

WHERE TO FIND:
Monarch butterflies are found near milkweed and other flowering plants in much of North America.

WHAT TO LOOK FOR:

✱ SIZE
The wingspan of a monarch butterfly is about four inches.

✱ COLOR
Its wings are orange or brownish orange, with dark lines and white spots.

✱ BEHAVIOR
It returns north in summer to mate.

✱ MORE
Monarch caterpillars feed on poisonous milkweed leaves. The insects taste bad to birds, their biggest enemies.

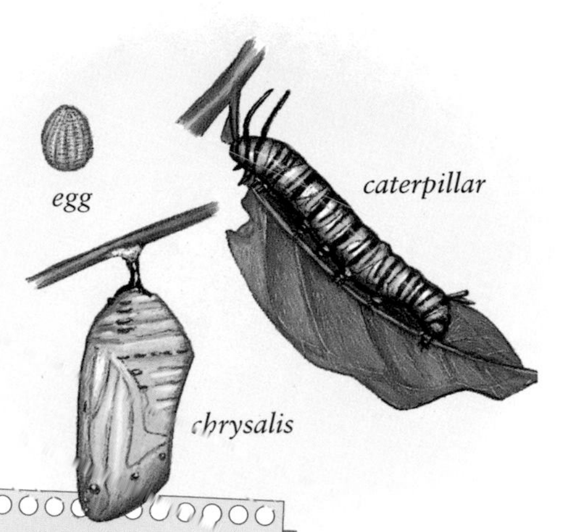

FIELD NOTES

Like all butterflies, monarchs change from egg to caterpillar to chrysalis (KRIH-suh-liss) to adult.

While monarchs feed on nectar from flowers, they pick up pollen on their bodies that is transferred to other flowers.

LUNA MOTH

BUSH-AND-SHRUB LEVEL

Like all moths, the elegant luna spends time as a hungry caterpillar. After it changes form into a moth, though, it does not eat during the rest of its one-week life.

Luna moths have large tails and feathery antennae that help them locate mates.

FIELD NOTES

Colorful marks called eye spots on this moth's wings frighten away enemies such as birds.

WHERE TO FIND: The luna moth lives mainly in deciduous forests in the eastern part of the United States.

WHAT TO LOOK FOR:

✱ SIZE
Luna moths have a wingspan of three inches, about the width of your palm.

✱ COLOR
They are a delicate pale green color.

✱ BEHAVIOR
Luna moth caterpillars munch leaves of walnut, hickory, birch, and other trees.

✱ MORE
The caterpillars are green, with yellow stripes, and are covered with prickly spines for protection from enemies.

BUMBLEBEE

BUSH-AND-SHRUB LEVEL

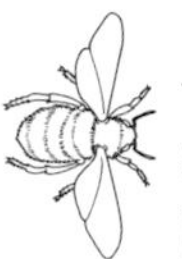

A queen bumblebee is pampered, surrounded by female worker bees and male bees called drones. Workers collect nectar and pollen and tend to her every need.

WHERE TO FIND:
Bumblebees are found in spring and summer on flowering plants throughout most of North America.

WHAT TO LOOK FOR:

✱ SIZE
Bumblebees are about one inch long.

✱ COLOR
These insects have furry bodies that are black, with yellow, or orange, or white.

✱ BEHAVIOR
Only the queen bee lays eggs in the colony.

✱ MORE
Bumblebees will sting attackers, such as birds or humans, to protect themselves. They can sting more than once.

FIELD NOTES

Stiff hairs on the bumblebee's rear legs gather pollen, which is carried in a kind of basket on each leg.

A bumblebee worker drinks sweet nectar from a flower. It will take the nectar back to the hive to feed the bees there.

FIREFLY

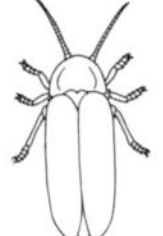

For many people, the yellow or green lights of fireflies at night signal the beginning of summer. The light comes from chemicals in the tip of the insect's abdomen.

WHERE TO FIND:
Fireflies are found on lawns, fields, and open woods in North America, from Canada southward.

WHAT TO LOOK FOR:

✱ **SIZE**
Fireflies range from ¼ to ¾ of an inch in length.

✱ **COLOR**
They have brown or black bodies, often with yellow or orange stripes.

✱ **BEHAVIOR**
In some firefly species, the adults do not eat during their short lives.

✱ **MORE**
Some kinds of fireflies eat snails, slugs, and even each other.

In the daytime, fireflies rest on the leaves of plants and bushes. They blend into the background and are hard to see.

FIELD NOTES

Male fireflies signal with their lights to wingless females on the ground. The females blink back.

BLACK-AND-YELLOW ARGIOPE

BUSH-AND-SHRUB LEVEL

The black-and-yellow argiope (are-JIE-uh-pee) isn't a shy spider. The female builds a web, parks in the center, and often bobs up and down while waiting for prey.

The spider's coloring resembles a yellow jacket's and may confuse its enemies.

WHERE TO FIND:

Black-and-yellow argiopes are found in meadows and gardens from southern Canada southward.

WHAT TO LOOK FOR:

✱ SIZE

Females range from ¾ to 1⅛ of an inch in length. Males are about half that.

✱ COLOR

These spiders have black bodies with yellow markings on the abdomen.

✱ BEHAVIOR

Females lay hundreds of eggs in a round sac at the edge of the web.

✱ MORE

After mating, the female eats the male. She dies after laying her eggs.

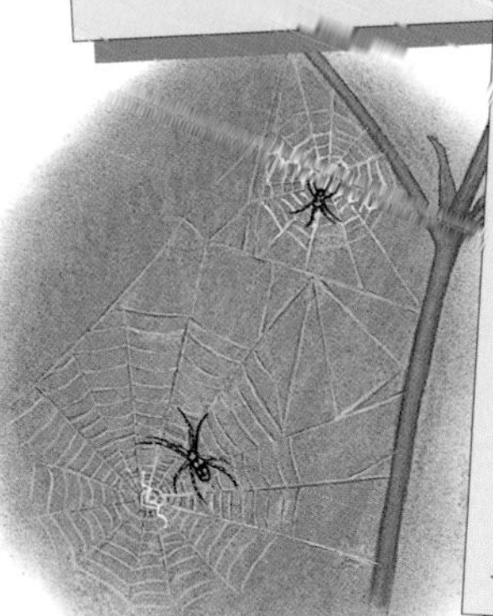

FIELD NOTES

The male spider spins his web at the edge of the female's, so he can be nearby at mating time.

SPIDER MITE

Bush-and-Shrub Level

Despite their tiny size, spider mites are real pests. They pierce plants with their sharp mouthparts and suck the juices out. This often causes the plants, such as your dad's prized roses, to weaken and die.

WHERE TO FIND:

Spider mites live in much of North America, feeding on plants in gardens, orchards, and even in houses.

WHAT TO LOOK FOR:

✱ SIZE
Spider mites are 1/64 to 1/32 of an inch long.

✱ COLOR
They are pale yellow, pale green, or pinkish, with spots.

✱ BEHAVIOR
Females spin loose webs of silk where they find shelter and lay their eggs.

✱ MORE
Mites are not insects. Mites are related to spiders and ticks. They have two-part bodies and eight legs.

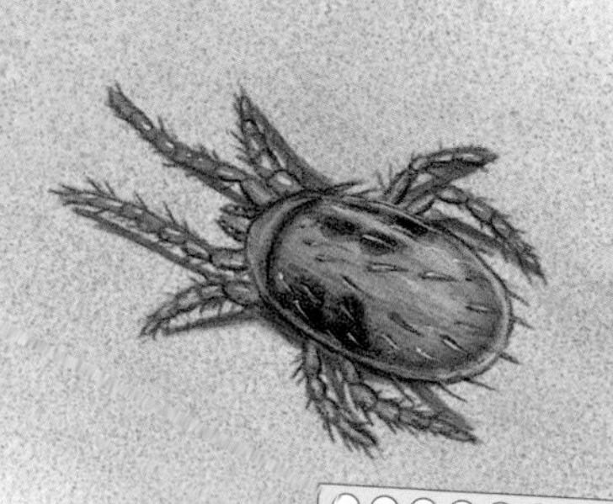

FIELD NOTES

The two-spotted spider mite was named for areas of undigested food that show through its clear abdomen.

A mass of spider mites swarming on a plant is very bad news for the plant's health.

GRAY SQUIRREL

TREE LEVEL

Gray squirrels sleep high in the trees at night. During the day they seldom stand still. They scamper up and down trees and across the ground. They dart about, searching for nuts and berries.

FIELD NOTES

Gray squirrels build large leaf nests, called drays, in the crooks of tree trunks or on branches.

Gray squirrels bury acorns. They usually dig up someone else's, finding them by smell, not memory.

WHERE TO FIND:

Gray squirrels are found in wooded areas in southeastern Canada and the United States.

WHAT TO LOOK FOR:

✷ SIZE

The gray squirrel measures about 20 to 25 inches long, including its tail.

✷ COLOR

It is gray above and paler below. Some are black.

✷ BEHAVIOR

Gray squirrels sometimes build nests in abandoned woodpecker holes.

✷ MORE

Some researchers think squirrels recover about 85 percent of buried nuts.

SOUTHERN FLYING SQUIRREL

TREE LEVEL

You may have a mammal living in your backyard you've never seen. Southern flying squirrels come out only at night, gliding from tree to tree in wooded areas.

WHERE TO FIND:

Southern flying squirrels are common in woodlands in most parts of the eastern United States.

WHAT TO LOOK FOR:

✷ SIZE
The southern flying squirrel is about ten inches long, including its tail.

✷ COLOR
It is grayish brown above and white below.

✷ BEHAVIOR
Like other squirrels, they often search the ground for nuts and seeds.

✷ MORE
Their large, round eyes help them see well at night.

A southern flying squirrel clings to a tree branch. A relative lives in the northern United States and Canada.

FIELD NOTES

The southern flying squirrel actually glides. It extends flaps of skin that act as a kind of parachute.

LITTLE BROWN BAT

TREE LEVEL

You will find the little brown bat here, there, and everywhere—if you look at night, when this small mammal is active. It flies low in the sky, in a kind of zigzag pattern, hunting for insects.

WHERE TO FIND:

Little brown bats are found in a variety of habitats throughout the central part of North America.

WHAT TO LOOK FOR:

✳ SIZE
Little brown bats are about four inches long, with ten-inch wingspans.

✳ COLOR
They are shiny brown with tan-colored chests and bellies.

✳ BEHAVIOR
Flying bats make a honking noise at each other to avoid midair collisions.

✳ MORE
Males roost by themselves, away from the nursery groups.

A little brown bat clings to the bark of a tree trunk, displaying the furry body that marks it as a mammal.

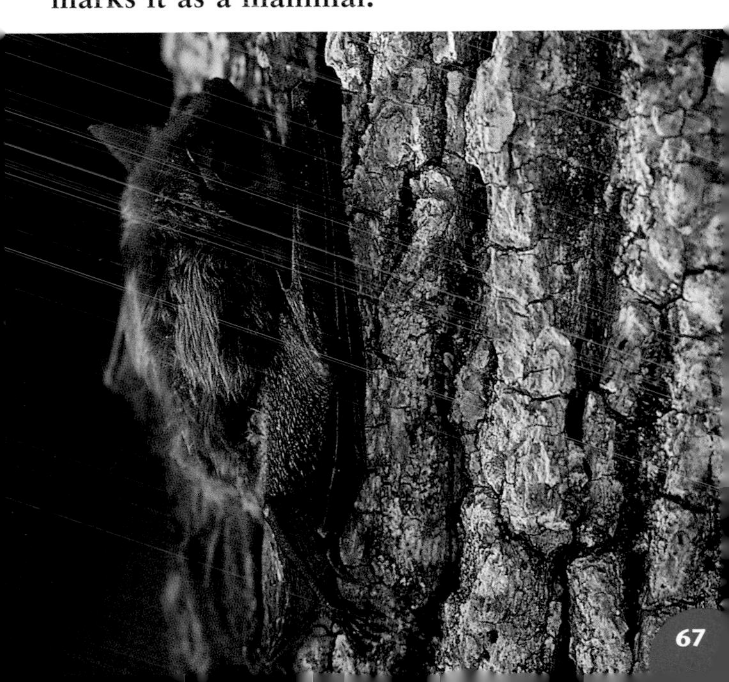

SCREECH-OWL

TREE LEVEL

The calls of screech-owls often add a spooky sound to the woods—or to your backyard—at night. Screech-owls really don't screech at all. They make a whistling kind of wail, often to attract mates.

WHERE TO FIND:

Eastern and western screech-owls live in many different habitats from Canada into Mexico.

WHAT TO LOOK FOR:

✱ SIZE
Screech-owls measure 8½ inches long.

✱ COLOR
Depending on where they live, screech-owls have grayish or reddish plumage.

✱ BEHAVIOR
They are sometimes seen during the day roosting in trees or at the entrance to their nest holes.

✱ MORE
They hunt for rodents, other small animals, and insects.

FIELD NOTES

Western screech-owls tend to be grayer than those in the east, which usually are more red in color.

A family of eastern screech-owls perch on a branch. They still wear some of the downy feathers of young birds.

NORTHERN CARDINAL

TREE LEVEL

With its bright red plumage and crest, the male northern cardinal is such a handsome bird that seven states have chosen the species as their state bird.

WHERE TO FIND:
Northern cardinals live in woods, swamps, and gardens from the eastern United States southward.

WHAT TO LOOK FOR:

✱ SIZE
Northern cardinals are almost nine inches long.

✱ COLOR
Males are red, with black faces and red bills. Females and young are brownish.

✱ BEHAVIOR
The northern cardinal crushes seeds—its favorite food—with its short, stout bill.

✱ MORE
Both males and females have crests and give loud, whistling calls.

A male northern cardinal folds down his crest and fluffs his feathers to keep warm in winter.

FIELD NOTES

When spring comes, cardinals pair up, singing and perching together in the budding trees.

DOWNY WOODPECKER

Tree Level

Some morning you may be awakened from a deep sleep by the sound of rapid tapping on wood. It might be a downy woodpecker, chipping into a tree to look for insects and spiders to eat.

Male downy woodpeckers have a red patch on the back of their head.

FIELD NOTES

These woodpeckers work very hard at excavating neat, round nest holes in the trunks of trees.

WHERE TO FIND:

Downy woodpeckers are found in parks, woods, yards, and orchards in central North America.

WHAT TO LOOK FOR:

✱ SIZE
Downy woodpeckers are nearly seven inches long.

✱ COLOR
They have black-and-white heads and white markings on their black wings.

✱ BEHAVIOR
Downies often eat at bird feeders.

✱ MORE
Animals that nest in trees like to move into old or abandoned woodpecker holes.

ACORN WEEVIL

TREE LEVEL

The acorn weevil is a kind of beetle with a long, thin snout. It feeds on and lays its eggs in acorns high in the branches of black, white, and red oak trees. It has wings, but seldom flies to the ground.

WHERE TO FIND:

Acorn weevils are found in deciduous forests in the eastern United States and as far west as Arizona.

WHAT TO LOOK FOR:

✱ SIZE
Acorn weevils are about ⅜ of an inch in length.

✱ COLOR
They have brown bodies, sometimes with tiny spots.

✱ BEHAVIOR
When an enemy threatens, a weevil may stay still, pretending to be dead.

✱ MORE
Males have curved snouts. Females' snouts are straighter.

FIELD NOTES

After hatching from an egg, an acorn weevil larva feeds on the acorn as it eats its way out.

The weevil uses her snout to drill a hole in an acorn so that she can lay her eggs inside.

GLOSSARY

abdomen On an insect, the rear segment of the body, which contains organs for digestion and reproduction.

amphibian An animal, such as a toad or salamander, that has skin without scales and lays its eggs in water.

antenna One of a pair of thin, segmented organs located on the head of an insect that help it smell, feel, and taste.

chrysalis The resting stage of a caterpillar as it transforms into an adult butterfly.

crop A pouch in the throat of many birds where food is temporarily stored and becomes softened.

crustacean A hard-shelled creature that usually lives in water and has many legs, such as a crab or crayfish.

deciduous Trees that shed all their leaves once a year.

habitat A plant or animal's natural place, such as a desert, a forest, or a river.

larva A stage in the life of many insects after hatching from an egg. A larva looks very different from an adult.

marsupial A mammal that is under-developed at birth and grows inside its mother's pouch, where it nurses until it can survive outside her body.

nectar The sugary liquid made in a flower that attracts insects and other animals that spread the flower's pollen.

pollen The fine, yellow powder made by flowers so they can reproduce.

reptile An animal that has scaly or leathery skin and usually lays eggs. Lizards and snakes are reptiles.

INDEX OF **BACKYARD WILDERNESS**

ABOUT THE CONSULTANTS

David W. Inouye is an ecologist and conservation biologist at the University of Maryland. He has studied insects and wildflowers at the Rocky Mountain Biological Laboratory since 1971. He researches ant-plant interactions and the bumblebees, hummingbirds, and flies that pollinate wildflowers that grow in the Colorado mountains.

Ronald M. Nowak worked as a mammalogist in the endangered species program of the U.S. Fish and Wildlife Service for 24 years. He is the author of the fourth, fifth, and sixth editions of *Walker's Mammals of the World,* and has published some 70 papers, articles, and books of scientific and popular interest.

George E. Watson served as Curator of Birds in the Smithsonian Institution's National Museum of Natural History from 1962 to 1985. A fellow and past secretary and vice president of the American Ornithologists' Union, he has been a member of the National Geographic Society's Committee for Research and Exploration since 1975.

PHOTOGRAPHIC CREDITS

Photographs supplied by Animals Animals/Earth Scenes.

front cover Fred Whitehead **back cover** Tom Ives **1** William Silliker, Jr. **2** Zig Leszczynski **7** Zig Leszczynski **9** G.R. Degginger **11** D.R. Spencer **13** Bill Beatty **15** Maresa Pryor **17** Alan G. Nelson **19** Ted Levin **20** Donald Specker **23** John Gerlack **25** Zig Leszczynski **27** Joe McDonald **29** Breck P. Kent **31** Breck P. Kent **33** Zig Leszczynski **35** Zig Leszczynski **37** Zig Leszczynski **39** Mark A. Chappell **41** Stan Schroder **43** Donald Specker **44** Michael Habicht **47** Conrad Kitsz **49** William D. Griffin **50** Robert Lubeck **53** Donald Specker **55** E.R. Degginger **57** James E. Lloyd **58** Donald Specker **61** Richard Shiell **63** Zig Leszczynski **65** Zig Leszczynski **67** Joe McDonald **69** Joe McDonald **70** Bates Littlehales **73** Tom Edwards **75** D. Wright / OSF **77** Zig Leszczynski **79** Richard Shiell